THE RESILIENT SLOTH

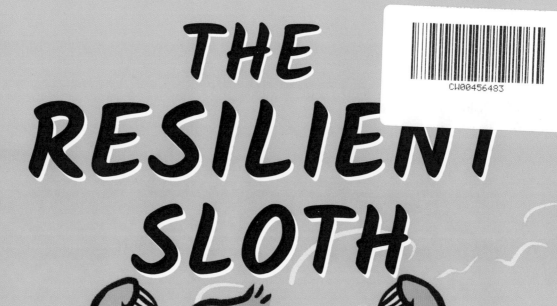

A Children's Book About Building Mental Toughness, Resilience, and How to Deal With Obstacles

ILLUSTRATED BY ADAM RIONG

WRITTEN BY CHARLOTTE DANE

Everyone that knew Sloth knew just how mentally tough he was. He never gave up or felt helpless! He felt like he could accomplish anything he put his mind to.

When Sloth struggled to learn how to play the guitar, he motivated himself by thinking,

Once Sloth hurt himself while playing baseball, and he dusted himself off and said to himself,

"I might have gotten hurt now, but once I heal I will be stronger and faster than before!"

And when Sloth lost a foot race to his friend Rabbit, he would think,

As a result, Sloth was always in a bad mood, which worried his parents. Sloth's friend Fox also noticed his behavior and knew just what would help him. He invited Sloth to come over to his house one night for a sleepover.

When they met, Fox took a sleepy Sloth outside to his telescope so that they could observe the faraway stars and planets together.

Fox told Sloth of a trick he often used when faced with various problems. He said, "I have been using something called the 10/10/10 rule whenever I feel myself being overwhelmed. Just like we see far into the distance with the telescope, all you need to do is look far into the future with your imagination."

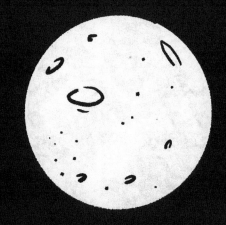

"Whenever you're faced with an issue ask yourself three things."

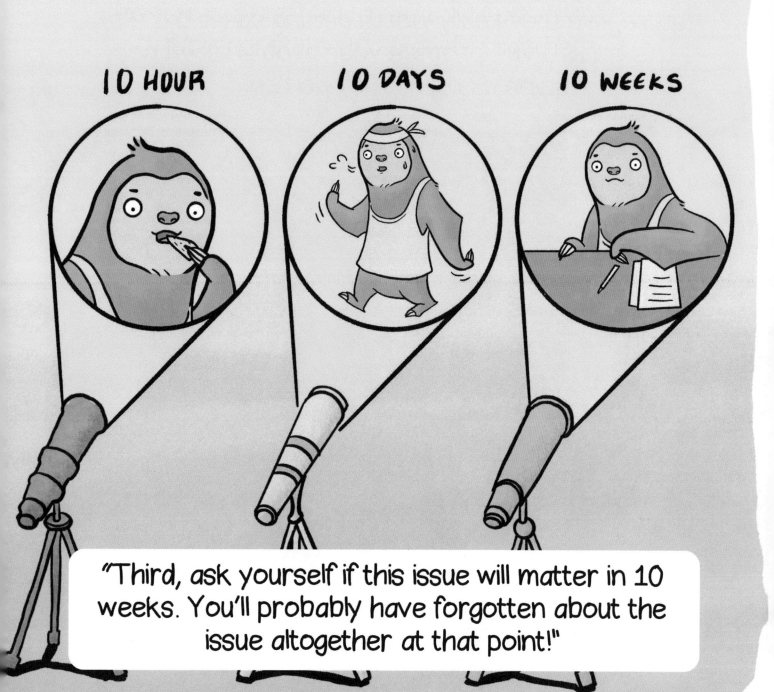

"Third, ask yourself if this issue will matter in 10 weeks. You'll probably have forgotten about the issue altogether at that point!"

"The important part is that we gain perspective that our emotions and feelings don't always accurately represent reality, and this helps us get through anything at all!"

Sloth was still doubtful of his friend's suggestion. Nevertheless, he promised to try and tell Fox how it went.

Can you guess what happened after Sloth asked himself these three questions? He felt confident that things would be fine if he got it wrong... and he even managed to get the right answer!

He vowed to worry less and not be as bothered by the problems that came his way. He just had to think about the future to see that his worries were not worth being overwhelmed over.

He applied the rule once again when he couldn't go out to play because his parents said no. Instead of becoming frustrated, he asked himself, "Will this matter in 10 hours? No, because I will be sleeping then. Will it matter in 10 days? No, I would have played with my friends several times by then!".

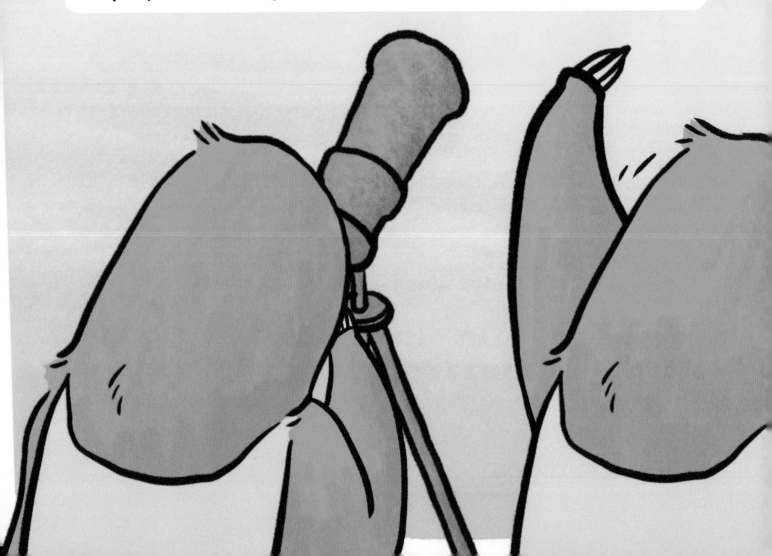

He did not even have to wonder about whether it would bother him after 10 weeks. Like before, Sloth successfully controlled his emotions and did not let small problems faze him.

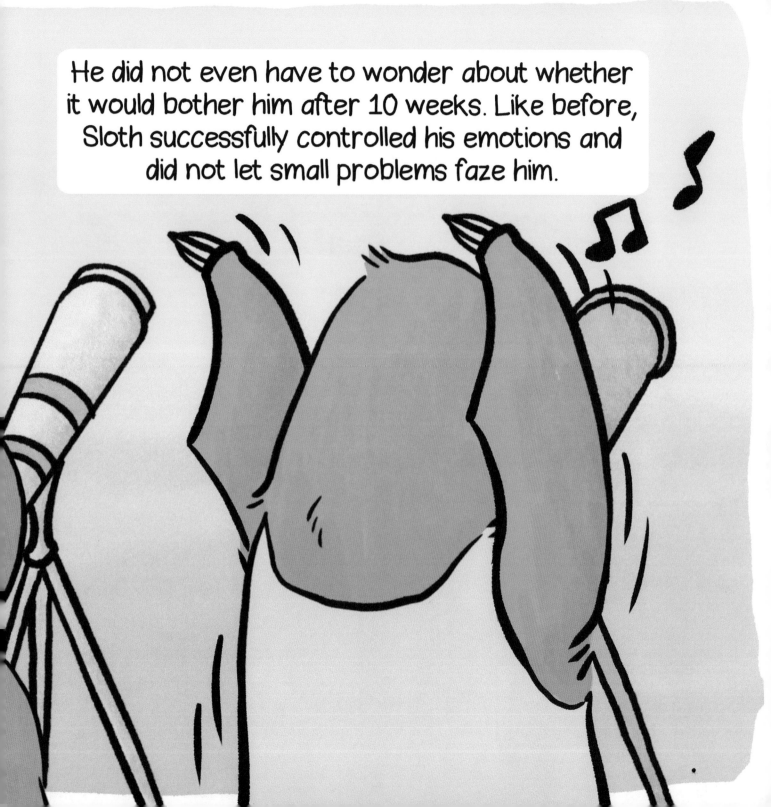

From that day onwards, Sloth would never forget to apply the 10/10/10 rule whenever he faced a challenge. He realized just how many issues did not even bother him after 10 hours, let alone 10 days and 10 weeks! All problems became small when you look at a longer length of time, and you realize how many things we can let go of and stop worrying about.

The 10/10/10 rule can help anyone in difficult situations develop mental toughness and resilience to successfully overcome their problems!

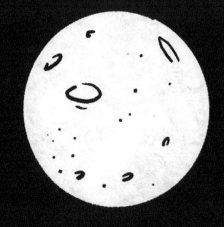

For more, visit
BigBarnPress.com